SONNY LEADS

To Ash! & Mark

Keep Kicking high!

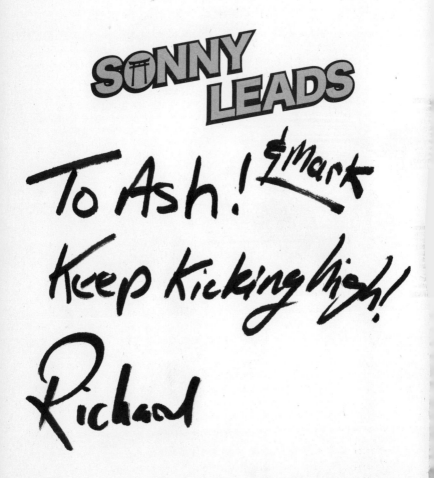

Richard

武道館
Japanime
TOKYO SAN FRANCISCO

story Richard Mosdell

SONNY LEADS

art Genshi Kamobayashi

Publisher's Note

This is a work of fiction. Names, characters, businesses, places, events and incidents are either the products of the author's imagination or used in a fictitious manner. Any resemblance to actual persons, living or dead, or actual events is purely coincidental.

That being said, every incident described in the story has been experienced by many non-Japanese in their own way as well as by local Japanese interacting with visitors from overseas. What is fascinating is that some of the more sensational moments portrayed in this fictional manga have actually happened under very similar circumstances to many people on a basis more regular than one would imagine.

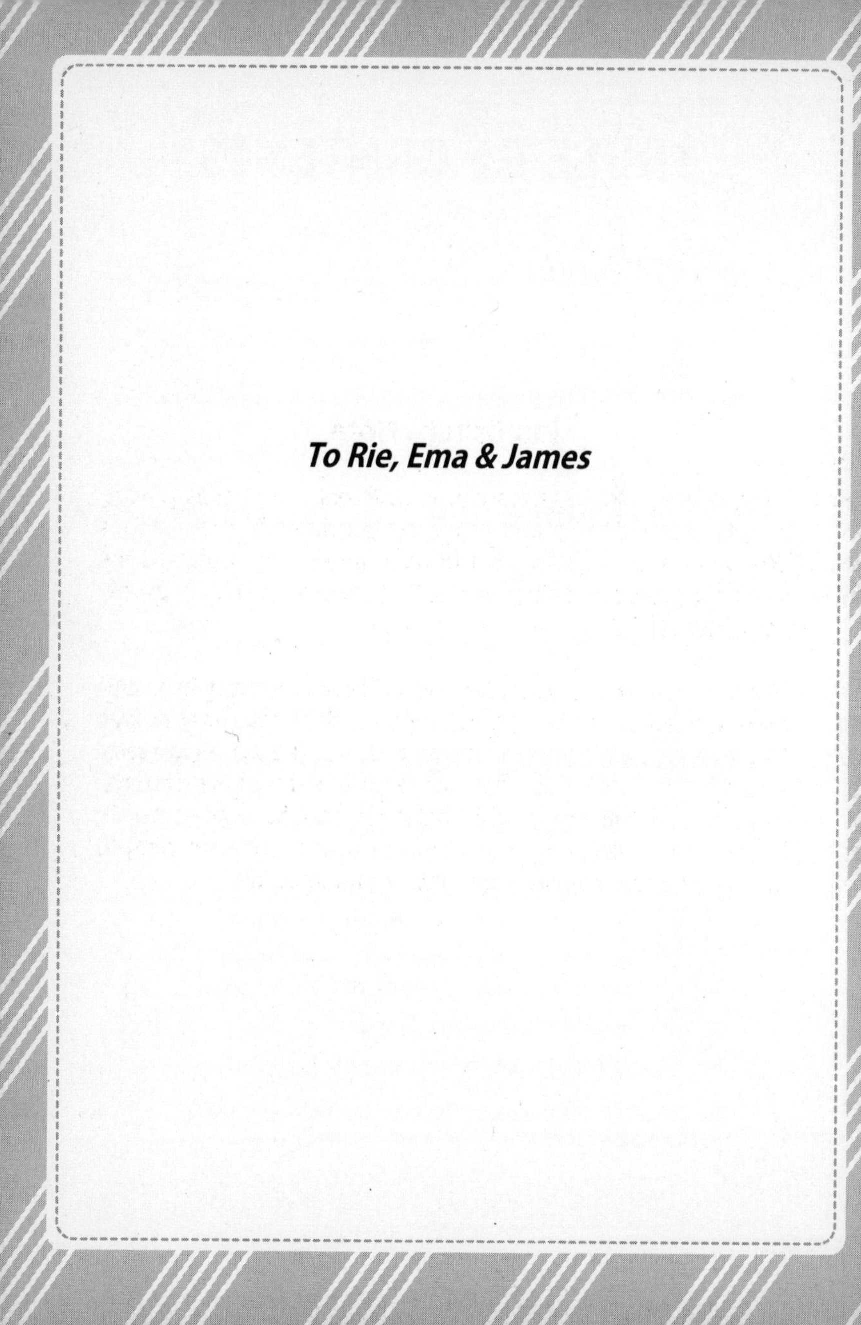

To Rie, Ema & James

TABLE OF CONTENTS

The material in the bonus section is presented Western-style, from left page to right.

Narita International Airport

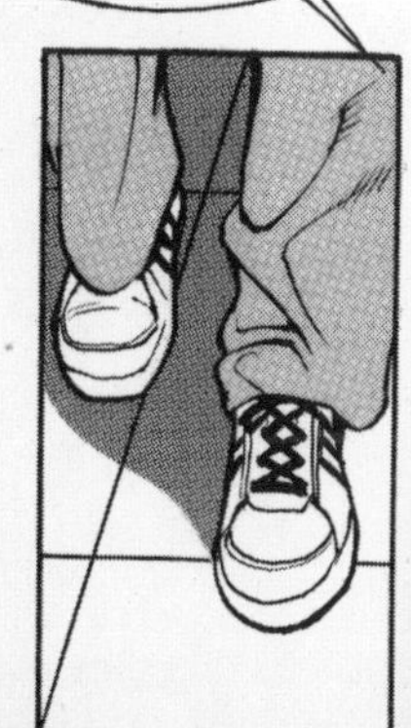

1 ARRIVAL

I'M HERE!
NOW, THE QUESTION IS... WILL THEY *ACTUALLY* LET ME IN?

HEY THERE! Meet Sonny Leads, a *karateka* with something to prove. To himself, and to the world. He just doesn't know it yet...

Two weeks ago...

HERE! THE GATEWAY TO THE FINALS!

KIAI!!!

World Karate Federation (WKF) rules: *Ippon* 3 points, *Wazari* 2 points, *Yuko* 1 point.

WAAAAAAAAA!
NOT AGAIN...
AHH!

AKA IPPON!
AKA NO KACHI!
IT'S NOT A PERSONAL BEST THIS YEAR, EH, SONNY?
NOPE, SAME RESULT. FOURTH. AGAIN. NO MEDAL, NO NATIONAL SQUAD QUALIFICATION.
IF YOU DO GO THROUGH ANOTHER YEAR OF TRAINING LIKE THE LAST TWO, YOU MIGHT MAKE IT HERE AGAIN.
THAT'S HARD TO HEAR, COACH.

WHO'S WHO: This coach trains the all-styles regional team. An instructor at a dojo is called "Sensei."

Back at the airport...

FAST FACT: Most Japanese know how to read and write English by the time they finish high school.

LONG FLIGHT. CAN'T WAIT TO SLEEP.
ファ〜

KAZ, WHERE ARE YOU TAKING US?

FIRST WE STOP AT THE DOJO IT FEELS RESPONSIBLE FOR YOU.
I'VE NEVER HAD A BUILDING FEEL RESPONSIBLE FOR ME BEFORE. HOW CONSIDERATE. BUT THE DOJO NEEDN'T WORRY...

I'LL BE FINE. I'M A BLACK BELT.

YOKO, YOU SPEAK ENGLISH VERY WELL.

REALLY? OH, THANK YOU! BUT NO, IT'S SO HARD FOR ME. KAZUHIRO-SAN LIVED OVERSEAS, AS YOU KNOW, BUT I CAN ONLY GO FOR A VERY SHORT VACATION. SO, HOW DID YOU TWO MEET?
HAH! HE DIDN'T TELL YOU?

HE WAS VISITING THE *MMA* CLUB NEXT TO MY DOJO...
BLAH, BLAH...

...WHEN THE DUDE ALMOST *KILLED* ME WITH HIS SKATEBOARD!
I WAS SO READY TO KICK HIS BUTT!
WHHHAAA!
YOSH!

NO WORRIES. SO, WHERE'S YOUR DOJO?

WHERE ELSE? JAPAN!

NO WAY! TELL ME *MORE!*

KAZU-CHAN WAS RIDING A *SKATEBOARD?*

YOKO, WHY DO PEOPLE IN JAPAN HANG THEIR LAUNDRY OUTSIDE?

THE LAND OF GIANT ROBOTS CAN'T AFFORD CLOTHES DRYERS?
NO ONE HERE HAS A DRYER. PLUS, CLOTHES DRY BETTER OUTDOORS. DO YOU HAVE LAUNDRY TO DO?

UH, NO. I JUST GOT HERE. RIGHT?
WELL, YOU CAN DO YOUR LAUNDRY TONIGHT AT YOUR HOMESTAY.

LAUNDRY NUTTER, HUH? OR DO I ALREADY STINK?
SNIFF, SNIFF

HOP OUT,
KID.
WE'RE HERE.

DID YOU KNOW? With more than 13 million residents, Tokyo is one of the most densely populated cities on the planet. But there is always room above an old warehouse for a karate dojo!

ギャハハ

HELLO!
MY NAME IS ICHIRO!
HAVE A NICE DAY!

THOSE ARE MEMBERS OF THE KIDS KARATE CLASS.

SONNY-KUN, THIS IS SUZUKI-*SENSEI*.
NICE TO MEET YOU, *SENSEI*.

LISTEN UP! Karate features countless battle cries. Kiai! Diai! Bua! Daa! Waa! Ai-ya! Ii-ya! Hi-sa! Yu-sa! Do you have a favorite?

SONNY IS MODEST? HAHA. FUNNY! MEN CHANGE RIGHT HERE. HURRY UP!
WHERE DO I GO TO CHANGE?
NOTHING TO SEE HERE, LADIES. MOVE ALONG...
クス
クス
KIAI!
BUUUAA!
ドッ
ドッ

PIECE OF CAKE.

HE'S GOT NO MOVEMENT, SO SLOW...

UMPH!

AI-YA!

FAST FACT: It is the explosive speed of the techniques that shocks newcomers, even when no contact is made.

キィーッ
adidas
BUNBU 押
BUNBU 押忍

オーーッス
文武大
文武大

BUNBU 押忍

WHO ARE *THESE* GUYS? I NEED TO REST!

AGAIN!
OSS!
TURN AROUND!

ONCE MORE!

HOW MANY TIMES DO WE HAVE TO DO THE SAME TECHNIQUE?

YAME! STOP!

修文練武

EVERYONE TAKE A SHORT BREAK.

BASIC... REPETITIVE... EXHAUSTING.

HOW'S JAPANESE KARATE, SONNY-KUN?

I CAN BARELY STAND...

LOOK, WE'VE DONE ONE STANDING PUNCH AND ONE LUNGE PUNCH, OVER AND OVER, FOR AN HOUR. ARE WE GOING TO BE HERE *ALL NIGHT?*

RESUME!
TURN AROUND! AND AGAIN!
RIIIIGHT...
NOT "WE." JUST YOU. HAHA. I AM FUNNY.
BEGIN!
KIAI!
AI-YA!

UMPH!
DON'T STOP!
MOVE!
NO WAY! TOO FAST!
YUUU...
IF THAT'S HOW IT WORKS, WELL, THEN...

...SAAAA!
AIIIII...
YA!
WHOAH, DUDE, I'M SORRY. I LOST CONTROL OF THAT KICK.
WHAT THE?! YOU *SO* MEANT TO DO THAT.

PIKO
HOLY DOUBLE DRILLS, CATWOMAN! AGAIN?
OSS! THAT'S IT FOR TONIGHT!

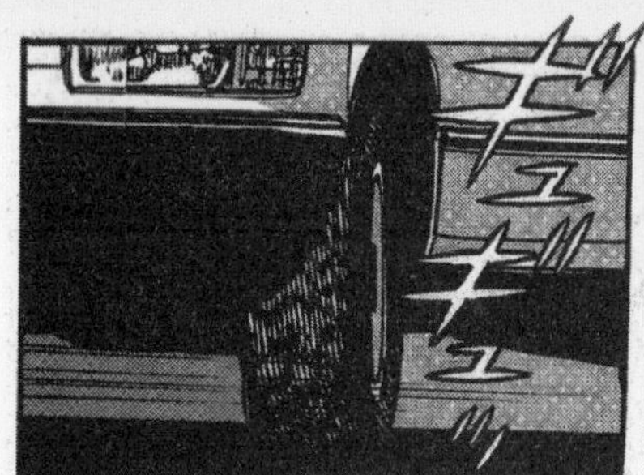

② HOMESTAY

田中

HEY KID, WAKE UP. END OF LINE. WE'RE HERE.

キッ

OOPS! SORRY?
OUCH! OOCH! EECH!
WELCOME! COME ON IN!

UH... DON'T EVERYONE TALK AT ONCE.

PLEASED TO MEET YOU, MRS. TANAKA.
YOKOSO, SONNY-KUN.. CALL ME OKAASAN.

SONNY, THIS IS MRS. TANAKA.
ハーイ

DOES HE THINK I'M GOING TO BEHAVE LIKE *HE* DID WHEN HE WAS IN *MY* COUNTRY?
VERY FUNNY, SKATEBOARD MAN...
ガ
SHE IS VERY HAPPY TO HAVE YOU AS A HOST STUDENT... SO BE A NICE BOY.

SONNY-KUN! SUCH A NICE BOY!

ERR, OKAASAN IS VERY BEAUTIFUL.

HEY, TARO, HOW'S IT GOIN'?

AND *HEEEEERE'S* TARO! HE'S 10 AND A TOP STUDENT IN SUZUKI-SENSEI'S KIDS CLASS.

DON'T BE TOO HAPPY NOW...

フン

ガハハハ
ORE! I'M *OTOOSAN.*
AND MR. TANAKA... ***OTOOSAN.***

I WILL EXPLAIN TO THE FAMILY THAT YOU WILL LOOK FOR WORK TEACHING ENGLISH.
BUT SINCE YOU CAN'T SPEAK JAPANESE, DON'T EXPECT TO EARN MUCH MONEY.

グビ

QUICK TIP: When visiting the home of a friend, always bring a small gift – *omiyage* – to show your gratitude for their hospitality.

SONNY,
DO YOU HAVE
LAUNDRY?

KARATE
DOGI, NE.
I'LL WASH
YOUR
DOGI
NOW.

OH, NO!
MY DOGI.
IT'S SWEATY
AND STAINED.
きゃあああ
プ
THEY'RE GONNA
FREAK OUT!
ガ

AH, SONNY. DOGI IS IN THIS BAG?

WHAAAAA?!?!

NO, NO!

I SHOULD DO IT!

IT'S OK!

シュワッチ

OYASUMI NASAI! GOOD NIGHT!
TANAKA-SAN, THANKS FOR TAKING CARE OF SONNY.

ブォー

TARO, LET'S GIVE SONNY A TOUR...

FOLLOW!

トイレ
LIFT! PUSH!

OTOOSAN AND OKAASAN IN HERE.
TARO ONLY!
タロウ

LET ME TAKE A PEEK... OMG!
空手道
ドン

バタン
HEY, WATCH THE DOOR!
SO SORRY ABOUT TARO...
MAMA

NOW SONNY'S ROOM.
NICE!

APPARENTLY I WON TROPHIES EVEN BEFORE I GOT HERE!

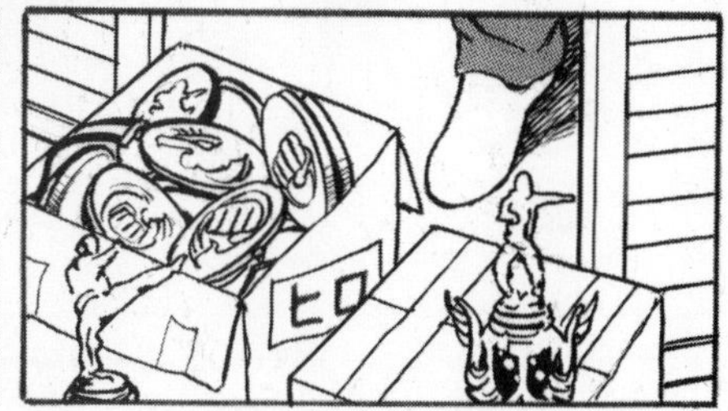

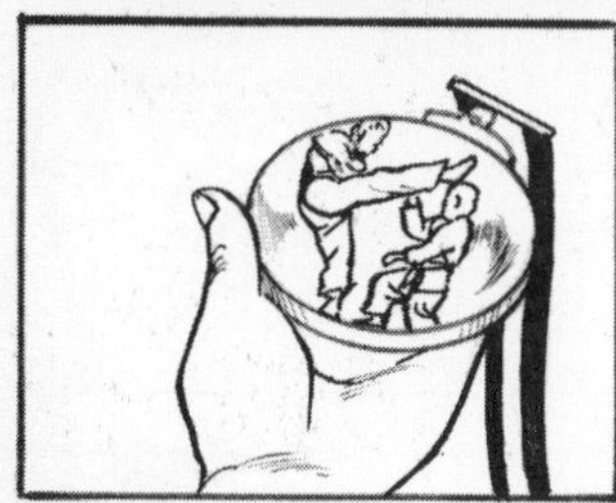

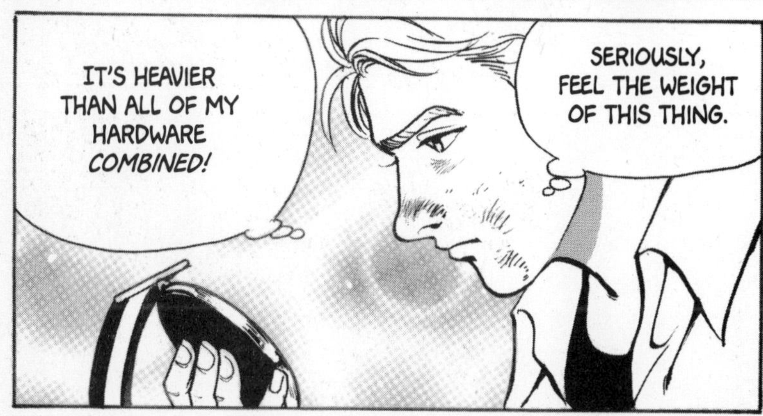
SERIOUSLY, FEEL THE WEIGHT OF THIS THING.
IT'S HEAVIER THAN ALL OF MY HARDWARE *COMBINED!*

SONNY... HOME, SWEET HOME?
ABSOLUTELY! THANK YOU. THIS ROOM IS GREAT.

BUT WHAT'S THE DEAL WITH THESE MEDALS?

タロウ
ニュッ
ニュッ
ニュッ

HATE GAIJIN MUCH? HE IS PROBABLY MIFFED I'M HERE, JUST STEWING...
"SO UNFAIR. NOT FAIR. MISSED THE LANDING FOR FAIR AND BOUNCED OFF THE CLIFF OF UNFAIR TO BURN AT THE BOTTOM."
HEY, I DIDN'T CHOOSE THIS HOMESTAY EITHER, LITTLE BUDDY.
ダン
バタン
THERE, THERE. BE STILL, MY LOVELIES.
段位証書
KAR

I'VE ALREADY SPENT SIX HOURS IN A DOJO. AND I GOT A BLOODIED NOSE - LOOK!
SO I MADE IT. ALL THE WAY. I'M REALLY HERE.

I'M PRETTY SURE THEY ARE PHOTOS OF THE OLDER SON. THE ROOM IS FILLED WITH KARATE TROPHIES, TOO.

BUT THEY HAVEN'T SAID ANYTHING ABOUT HIM.

MAYBE HE THREW A KILLING KICK AT A TOURNAMENT AND WAS KICKED OUT IN SHAME.

NO, THEY EXILED HIM FROM THE COUNTRY FOR COMMITTING SUCH A GREAT DISHONOR!

SPOOKY. FOR SURE TRUE.

NOW HE'S WALKING THE EARTH, REFLECTING ON HIS WORTHINESS, MEETING FRIEND AND FOE.
ヒロ

IS HIS PICTURE CUTE?
ヒロ
メダル
OR PROBABLY HE'S JUST AT SOME JAPANESE UNIVERSITY AND LIVING IN A DORM.

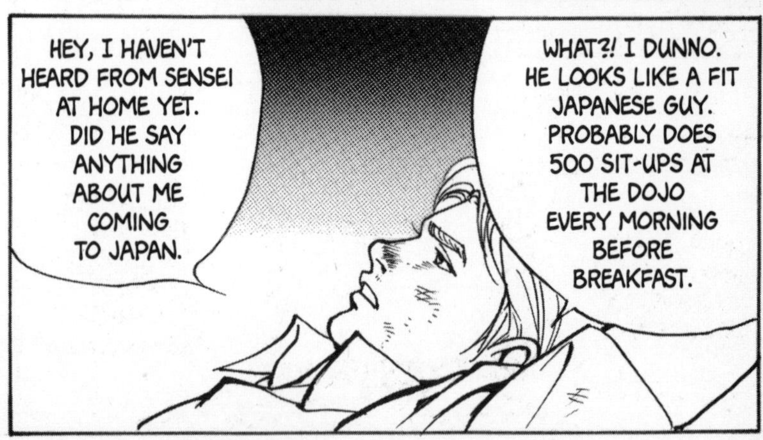
HEY, I HAVEN'T HEARD FROM SENSEI AT HOME YET. DID HE SAY ANYTHING ABOUT ME COMING TO JAPAN.
WHAT?! I DUNNO. HE LOOKS LIKE A FIT JAPANESE GUY. PROBABLY DOES 500 SIT-UPS AT THE DOJO EVERY MORNING BEFORE BREAKFAST.

ACTUALLY, HE SAID HE HAD JUST MISSED A CALL FROM MASTER USOYAJI, WHO LEFT HIM A CRYPTIC VOICEMAIL MESSAGE.
YOU TOOK YOUR OFFICIAL DAN CERTIFICATES WITH YOU, RIGHT?
段位証書
YEP, LET'S JUST HOPE THEY DON'T TAKE ONE LOOK AT MY FORM AND SAY...

"NO, NO, YOU SHOULDN'T BE HAVING THOSE. WE'LL JUST TAKE THEM BACK FROM YOU."

YOU DID GET YOUR NIDAN DIRECTLY FROM MASTER, SO MAYBE THEY'LL SAY...
"OOOH, NOW THAT'S WHAT A NIDAN IS SUPPOSED TO LOOK LIKE."

OH YEAH, EXACTLY! "MR. SONNY-KUN, A *NIDAN* IS SO BENEATH YOU. HERE IS A *GODAN*, NO HARD FEELINGS.'
HOLD ON... YOU KNOW HOW MUCH I ADMIRE YOUR TALENT, BUT....

AND IF I SUCK? THEY MIGHT THINK I EXPERTLY FORGED MY CERTIFICATES IN PHOTOSHOP.

WHEN HAVE YOU EVER DONE ***ANYTHING*** *EXPERTLY?*
RIGHT! I NEVER COULD PULL ONE OVER ON YOU!

SONNY?

...FROM THE MASTER'S VOICEMAIL.

SONNY?

3 TRAINING DAY

SO BEING 2 MINUTES LATE MEANS YOU'RE 3,840 KILOMETERS BEHIND.
LET'S GO.
ダンス
空手道
師範
鈴木七段
ヨガ
SUZUKI SENSEI WANTS TO EXAMINE YOUR DAN CERTIFICATES.
IS SOMETHING WRONG?

ARE THESE YOUR ORIGINALS? YOU GOT THEM DIRECTLY FROM YOUR SENSEI?
MY SENSEI'S SENSEI, MASTER USOYAJI, GAVE THEM TO EVERYONE.

SEE, THERE... SIGNED BY MASTER USOYAJI...
...AND THAT'S THE ASSOCIATION NUMBER.

BUT THESE WERE ALSO SIGNED BY AN ASSOCIATION PRESIDENT WHO DIED TEN YEARS AGO, WHICH IS KINDA WEIRD.

OH, THAT... WE WERE TOLD THEY LEAVE THE SIGNATURE ON OUT OF RESPECT TO THE FORMER PRESIDENT.

AH...
JUST A SEC.
......
....
......

LET'S GO, GAIJIN-SAN.

WHAT DID SUZUKI SENSEI SAY?
YOU MEAN, WHAT DID HE *NOT* SAY...

HUH? WHAT ARE *YOU* NOT SAYING?

PAYDIRT! Mrs. Tanaka has arranged for Sonny to meet the principal of an elite *juku* – cram school – that has a part-time job opening.

SO, DO YOU GET ALONG WITH CHILDREN?
YEAH, KIDS ARE GREAT!

NICE TO MEET YOU, MR. SONNY.
YOU, TOO.

AND CAN YOU PLAY SOCCER?
WELL, YES... BUT MY SPECIALTY IS KARATE.

UM, YES? OK, NOT VERY WELL.

OH, REALLY? AND CAN YOU DRAW PICTURES?

THAT'S OK.
YOU'LL BE FINE.
PLEASE COME HERE
EVERY WEEKDAY
FOR TWO HOURS.
NOON TO 2 P.M.

WHAT WILL
I DO?
TEACH
THE KIDS
ENGLISH?
NOT EXACTLY.
YOU'LL RIDE
THE JUKU BUS
AND GREET
THE STUDENTS
IN ENGLISH...

...AND HERE
AT THE JUKU
YOU'LL PLAY
SOCCER
AND OTHER
GAMES
WITH THEM.

THAT'S FINE, BUT, UM, HOW MUCH, LIKE, DO I GET PAID?
SOUNDS LIKE A PIECE OF CAKE. IT'S PROBABLY A VOLUNTEER POSITION...

I'M SORRY, BUT WE CAN'T PAY MUCH. IS 10,000 YEN PER DAY OK?

WOW!
10,000 YEN FOR 2 HOURS?!
THERE'S GOTTA BE A CATCH...

DIAPER CHANGING? NAH, THESE KIDS ARE TOO OLD FOR DIAPERS...

I BELIEVE I CAN ACCEPT THESE TERMS.
THERE'S NO DIAPER CHANGING REQUIRED, RIGHT?

YO!

HITS.
KEI-WAN!
HITSU!
HI-TSU?

GREEEEAT.
ALL GUYS
ARE ALIKE.
AH, THIS NUTTER
CALLS HIMSELF
"HITS" BECAUSE
HE LIKES TO
HIT PEOPLE
LIKE IN K-1.

Hitsu and Mr. Nice are protypical Japanese alpha males – the sort of guys you spar with, drink with ... and sometimes have to work with.

SURPRISE! If you hear kids on a playground yell "KANCHO!" (enema), it means someone has fallen victim to a popular anal-probe prank.

SONNY, TAKE OFF YOUR COAT AND PREPARE TO PLAY WITH THE CHILDREN.
YA-HO! SONNY SENSEI!

KAN....

WHO JUST CALLED ME "SENSEI?" YOU HAVE TO BE AN *OLD* DUDE TO BE A SENSEI!

...CHO!!!

ハアーーイ

A *hanko* is a rubber stamp used for signing official papers.

SONNY, HERE.
SIGN.

OK?
WOW,
THAT'S COOL!

NO,
NOT YET.
YES, YOUR
NAME IN
KATAKANA.
SONNY,
DO YOU KNOW
KATAKANA?

AND IS THIS
MY NAME?
名前
印
サニー

...NOT YET.
THAT'S OK.
SEE YOU!

AH,
*MADA DESU
NE...*

SONNY, LET'S GO! A NEW DOJO IS WAITING...
キ
IT'S ONLY BEEN 24 HOURS SINCE I GOT OFF THE BOAT. AND THIS IS SUPPOSED TO BE THE EASY DAY?!

4 DOJO MOJO

GREAT! NOW I CAN REALLY GET INTO IT...

IF I CAN STAY AWAKE.

TONIGHT IS ADULTS ONLY. DIFFERENT SENSEI.
SAME STYLE, THOUGH.

OGAMI SENSEI: aka "The World's Most Interesting Karate Instructor"

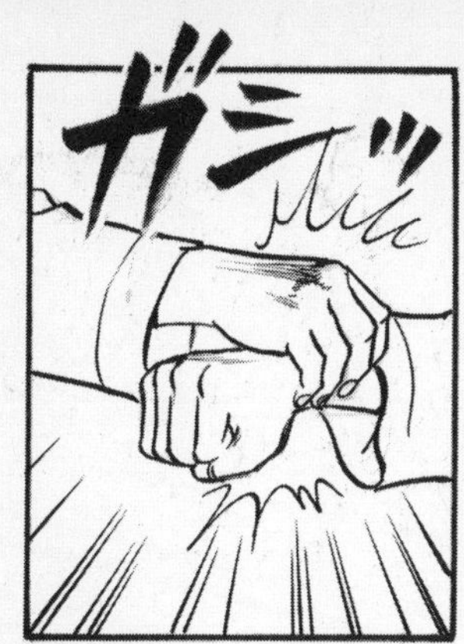
ガシッ

ICHI!

WHAT THE?!

YEAH! OOH, THAT FEELS BETTER.

MAN... THAT SLIDES FORWARD SO MUCH BETTER...
CHIGAU. WRONG.
CHIGAU!
WRONG!

CHIGAU!
IS THAT ALL HE CAN SAY?
TELL ME *WHAT* IS WRONG!
KAZUHIRO-KUN!
HAI!

AH,
CRAP...
SENSEI APPARENTLY HATES ME.
CAN'T A FELLA GET A BREAK?!

EH?
OH, WOW. LOOK AT THAT...

AI!
I'M IN LOVE...
NO, NO, SONNY. YOU CAN'T FALL FOR SOMEONE IN THE DOJO.
BUT... DAMN!
SONNY! GET BACK IN HERE!

HRRRMMMM!

大
大神

THIS WAY?
MO ICHIDO! ONCE MORE!

BUT WHY...?

AND AGAIN!

JUST TRY TO SUCKER-PUNCH ME AGAIN...
I DARE YOU.

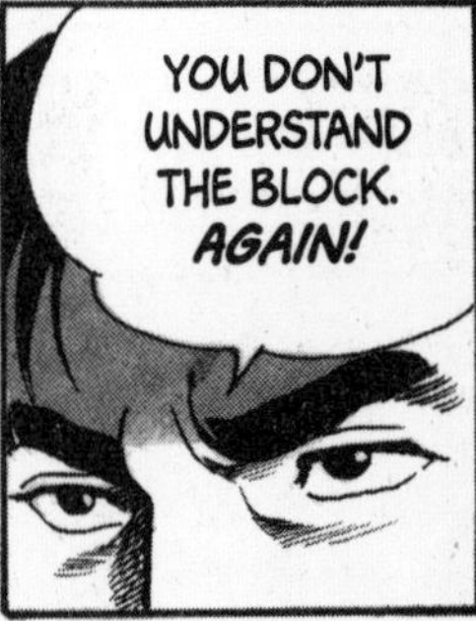
YOU DON'T UNDERSTAND THE BLOCK. *AGAIN!*

IT'S NOT THE SAME HERE AS IT IS AT HOME... IT IS *BETTER.*

NO... WAIT, SONNY, GROW UP...
YOU CAME HERE TO LEARN, TO GET BETTER, TO HAVE YOUR *JAPAN EXPERIENCE.*

UGH!

NO,
THIS WON'T
BREAK
YOU... ME...

DOUBLE
DARE YOU!
WHAT THE...?

ガクッ

YAME.
STOP.

YA-SHA!

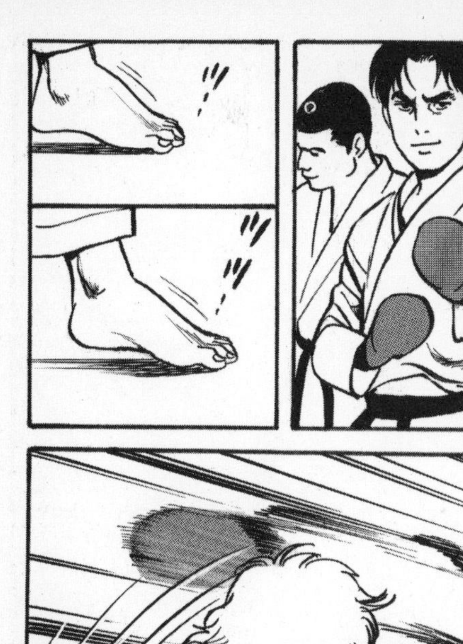

AI!

WAH!

ヌッ
ドオッ

WHAT THE?!

TIME FOR POST-WORKOUT REFRESHMENTS!
SONNY, LET'S GO.

HAS EVERYONE BACK HOME FORGOTTEN ABOUT ME?

AH, PLEASE LOOK THIS WAY. HMM... OH YEAH, GREETINGS IN JAPAN ARE HUGELY IMPORTANT.

ぎょうざ

ARIGATOU! THANKS!
UH, HEY... YOUR KATA IS GOOD... *KATA JOUZU!*

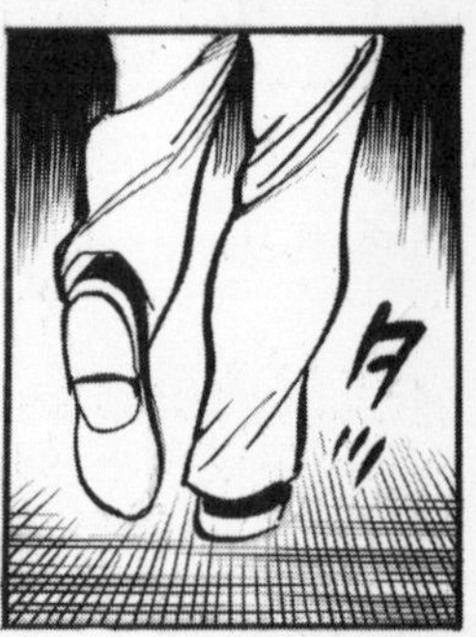

ハルカ
WHADDYA WANT?

I MEAN, *REALLY* GOOD.

UH-OH, HERE WE GO...
JUST THAT YOUR KATA IS GOOD. UNSU, RIGHT?
THANKS. BUT REALLY, WHAT DO YOU WANT?

WHERE YOU FROM?
AMERICAN, RIGHT?
NO, AUSTRALIAN.
BRITISH!

I'M SAYA!
I'M CHIE!
UM, I'M SONNY.

LIKE SONNY BONO? "I GOT YOU BABE" SONNY?

THWACK!

NO, NO, I GOT IT... HIS PARENTS WERE SONNY CHIBA FANS!

HOW DO YOU TWO KNOW ALL THAT STUFF?

WE ATTEND NIPPON INTERNATIONAL UNIVERSITY. ALL OF OUR CLASSES ARE TAUGHT IN ENGLISH. MY MAJOR IS AMERICAN POP CULTURE FROM 1978 TO 1988.
AND MINE IS GLOBAL SECURITY TREATIES THAT LED TO THE END OF THE COLD WAR.
KOKI

GOTTA GO. SEE YOU, SONNY!
SATURDAY, *NE!*
COFF

HARU-CHAN!

I DON'T KNOW IF THEY'RE THE ONES WHO ARE CRAZY... OR IF IT'S ME.
SONNY, IT'S PARTY TIME!

⑤ REALITY CHECK

SONNY-KUN. BOKU GA OGAMI DESU. I AM OGAMI.

OGAMI SENSEI IS A FAMOUS INSTRUCTOR IN YOUR STYLE. HE WAS JAPAN CHAMPION BACK IN COLLEGE.
GAMI
場

Japanese partygoers traditionally offer a round of applause after taking their first drinks following a toast.

I THINK HE IS HALF. HIS DAD WAS JAPANESE, I BELIEVE.

HMMM, "USOYAJI." IS HE JAPANESE?
HE AND MY INSTRUCTOR ARE CLOSE. I'VE SEEN HIM A DOZEN TIMES THE PAST 10 YEARS.

LOTS OF FITNESS DRILLS MIXED WITH DOING KATA.
A VERY HARD DAN TEST...

HOW DID YOU EARN YOUR CERTIFICATES?

ムグムグ
AND DID USOYAJI SENSEI EXPLAIN HOW EXACTLY YOUR DOJO IS CONNECTED TO THE JAPAN ASSOCIATION?

IT TOOK LIKE 3 HOURS.

IN OUR ASSOCIATION, WE PAY $50 A YEAR...
ブルル
...THAT'S FOR MEMBERSHIP IN THE JAPAN ASSOCIATION.
HOLD ON, I'VE GOT A CALL...

YO, SONNY HERE. PERFECT TIMING!
KAZ IS HERE ASKING ME ABOUT MY CERTIFICATES.
THE JAPAN ASSOCIATION JUST NEEDS TO CHECK ITS LIST OF PERFECT NIDANS. I SCORED A 100 ON MY DAN TEST.
SONNY, THAT'S ACTUALLY WHY I'M CALLING YOU.
GREAT, FIRE AWAY!

SENSEI, THESE ARE SONNY'S CERTIFICATES...

OGAMIDO

SONNY, ABOUT THESE SIGNATURES...

EVERY ASSOCIATION HAS A SPLIT WHEN THE FOUNDER DIES. SO IT WAS OUR TURN, HUH?
THERE'S SOME SORT OF POLITICAL PROBLEM WITH JAPAN.

MASTER IS WORRIED YOU MIGHT GET CAUGHT UP IN A POLITICAL SCANDAL.
YOU DON'T SAY.

YEAH... SIGNED BY THE FORMER PRESIDENT AND THE FORMER CHIEF INSTRUCTOR.

"KARATE ORDER?" WHAT'S THAT? SOUNDS SERIOUS.
MASTER HAS A "KARATE ORDER" FOR YOU.

BUT SONNY, THIS CERTIFICATE WAS SIGNED SEVERAL YEARS AGO.
SO? THEY SIGN BLANKS ALL THE TIME FOR A LICENSED GRADER LIKE MASTER USOYAJI TO HAND OUT.

BOTH OF THOSE MEN DIED OF OLD AGE OVER TEN YEARS AGO.
GO ON...
TO PROTECT YOU FROM SCANDAL, THE ORDER PROHIBITS YOU FROM DOING ANY KARATE IN JAPAN.
YOU'VE GOT TO BE KIDDING!
SONNY, YOUR CERTIFICATES ARE *FAKES!*
SAY WHAT AGAIN?!?!
THAT'S RIGHT. SENSEI IS ALSO CONFUSED. THE ONLY OTHER THING MASTER TOLD HIM WAS THAT HE WOULD EXPLAIN MORE WHEN YOU RETURN.
BUT THAT DOESN'T MAKE ANY SENSE...

SONNY, USOYAJI IS A *FRAUD*. THE ASSOCIATION HAS NEVER HAD AN OFFICIAL BY THAT NAME.
THE ONLY REASON I CAME TO JAPAN WAS TO DO KARATE, UNDER THE GUIDANCE OF THE JAPANESE ASSOCIATION!
SONNY?
DON'T DO KARATE IN JAPAN?!
MY CERTIFICATES ARE FAKES?!
WHERE'S MY OXYGEN MASK?
LADIES AND GENTLEMEN, WE HAVE JUST LOST ALL CABIN PRESSURE.
USOYAJI IS A FRAUD?

SUZUKI SENSEI SENT YOUR CERTIFICATES TO THE HEAD OFFICE TO BE CHECKED. THE NUMBERING SYSTEM WAS ODD...
FOREIGN-ISSUED CERTIFICATES HAVE ENGLISH ON THEM, SO HE THOUGHT MAYBE THE NUMBERS WERE ONLY FOR OVERSEAS ASSOCIATIONS.

BUT THE HEAD OFFICE CONFIRMED THEY ARE BOGUS.
EVEN THE HANKO'S WRONG.
HANKO?
IT'S LIKE A NAME STAMP.
ARE YOU HEARING ALL OF THIS?

YEAH. EVERY WORD. WOW.
WHEN ISSUED BY THE HEAD OFFICE, THE BOTTOM HALF OF THE HANKO...
...IS STAMPED ON THE CERTIFICATE, AND THE UPPER HALF IS STAMPED IN THE OFFICIAL REGISTRATION BOOK.
KID, THESE AREN'T EVEN *GOOD* FAKES...

NONE OF THAT WAS FAKE! IT SHOULD STILL COUNT...

BUT I PASSED MY SHODAN AND NIDAN TESTS...
I SCORED A PERFECT 100!

THEY TOLD US BACK HOME WE WERE MEMBERS OF THE JAPANESE GROUP!
NO ONE FROM YOUR COUNTRY IS LISTED. AND DEAD MEN CAN'T SIGN CERTIFICATES.
KARATE

BUT THAT WAS THE BIG SELLING POINT OF OUR DOJO, THAT WE WERE LEGITIMATE!
THEY LIED.
OH MY GOD, THIS IS UNBELIEVABLE! BUT, THEN AGAIN... IT KIND OF EXPLAINS A LOT...
DID YOU HEAR THAT, TOO?
HOLD ON, SENSEI JUST ARRIVED.
KARATE

LET ME TALK TO HIM...
SENSEI IS THE MAN, HE'S WHY I STAYED IN THE DOJO...
I SHOULD LEAVE IT UP TO HIM.
SONNY, HOW'S JAPAN?
SENSEI, UM, WELL, I'M STILL HERE, BUT I'M CONFUSED.
WHAT DO YOU THINK I SHOULD DO?
I DON'T UNDERSTAND ALL THE FUSS, BUT YOU'RE THERE NOW. SO JUST DO EVERYTHING YOU WANT TO DO, LEARN EVERYTHING YOU CAN...
IF MASTER COMPLAINS, I'LL TAKE THE HEAT. ENJOY JAPAN. FOCUS ON JAPAN. WE'LL BE HERE WHEN YOU GET BACK.
OK, THANKS.
SONNY, I'M BACK. SENSEI LOOKS AS CONFUSED AS YOU PROBABLY DO RIGHT NOW.
I'LL BET! GOTTA GO NOW...
SO, YOU'RE NOT SUPPOSED TO TRAIN IN JAPAN?
SOUNDS LIKE SOMETHING A CULT LEADER WOULD SAY.

THERE ARE NO POLITICAL PROBLEMS SPLITTING THE ASSOCIATION HERE. THAT HAPPENED 30 YEARS AGO WHEN SOME SMALLER GROUPS OF DOJO LEFT. BUT THE ASSOCIATION IS STILL WHOLE.
SURE, SOME PERSONALITIES DON'T LIKE ONE ANOTHER, BUT THAT'S NORMAL IN ANYTHING.

MY SENSEI SAID I SHOULD JUST TRAIN, ENJOY JAPAN AND LEARN EVERYTHING I CAN.

OSS! THAT'S RIGHT. KARATE IS *NOT* A CULT.
DRINK UP! MORE DRINKS FOR SONNY!!

THIS IS *SOOOOOOO* GOOD!

OOOOF!

KAZUHIRO...

CRIKEY, THAT HURTS! I JUST FOUND OUT I'M A FAKE BLACK BELT IN A FAKE ASSOCIATION! NO NEED TO HIT ME.

SONNY, GOOD KICK!
SONNY, GOOD PUNCH!

SONNY, OGAMI SENSEI SAYS YOU NEED TO BE REBORN.

SO KAZ-SAN, WHAT DOES BEING REBORN *REALLY* MEAN FOR ME?
AM I A WHITE BELT ALL OVER AGAIN?

グビー

ワハハ
JK

I WILL TRANSLATE FOR OGAMI SENSEI:
"WHY ARE YOU HERE? TO LEARN KARATE? WHY ARE *YOU* HERE?"

HE SAYS, "HMM. SONNY, YOU WILL THEN GO HOME SOON?"
WELL, I'VE ALWAYS WANTED TO EXPERIENCE KARATE IN JAPAN.

HE ASKS, "THAT'S IT? THEN WHY NOT GO TO EUROPE? THEY HAVE STRONG KARATAKA AND FAMOUS DOJOS, TOO."

NO, I WANT TO STAY AND STUDY AND LEARN AND EXCEL UNTIL...
UNTIL I'M A *CHAMPION!*

IT'S BEEN MY DREAM TO COME HERE EVER SINCE...
"SINCE YOU STARTED LOOKING AT JAPANESE GIRLS ON THE INTERNET? YOU WANT A JAPANESE GIRL?"

HE STILL DOUBTS YOUR MOTIVES. "MAYBE YOU LOVE ANIME AND MAID CAFES?"

NO! I'M HERE BECAUSE I NEEDED TO CHANGE MY APPROACH TO TRAINING SO I CAN WIN MY COUNTRY'S OPEN-STYLE NATIONALS.

NO, OGAMI SENSEI. NO! BELIEVE ME, THAT'S NOT IT AT ALL!
WHEN I WAS A KID, OUR FAMILY HAD A JAPANESE HOMESTAY STUDENT. WE CALLED HIM "JC." HE INTRODUCED ME TO KARATE, AND MY PARENTS ENROLLED ME IN THE ONLY DOJO IN TOWN CONNECTED TO JAPAN.

OGAMI SENSEI SAYS YOUR CASE IS NOT UNCOMMON, SONNY. MANY OVERSEAS CLUBS USED TO BE PART OF THE JAPAN GROUP, BUT OVER THE YEARS THEY DRIFTED AWAY.

MORE THAN ANYTHING.

OH? BUT WHAT DO I DO NOW?
SENSEI ASKS, "DO YOU REALLY WANT TO BE A KARATEKA?"

"DO YOU PROMISE NOT TO GIVE UP EVEN WHEN YOU FEEL YOU ARE FAILING?"

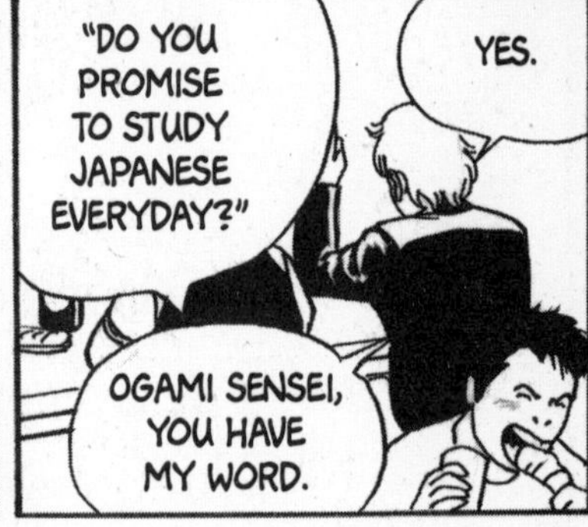
YES.
"DO YOU PROMISE TO STUDY JAPANESE EVERYDAY?"
OGAMI SENSEI, YOU HAVE MY WORD.

"THEN YOU SHALL RETEST YOUR SHODAN IN 3 MONTHS, AND YOUR NIDAN AFTER THAT. GAMBATTE!"

HEY, KAZ... WHAT'S WITH THE OJ?
DESIGNATED DRIVER.
TONIGHT IS NOT ABOUT ME, SONNY. TONIGHT IS ABOUT YOU! YOU ARE NOW A MEMBER OF *OUR* GROUP.
Orange
100

It is customary for a host to end a party with a cry of "Yoh-oi!" Everyone then applauds in successive bursts of three claps.

SONNY, *DAIJOBU?*
HE STINKS!

RIGHT-O! *I STINK!*

I STINK *SO BAD,* I'M A WHITE BELT AGAIN...

OUCH!

OH, MAN...
...OH, MAAAN.

WAH! TOO BRIGHT!

SONNY?
SONNY?!
SONNY!!!

WHO'S THERE?
SONNY!

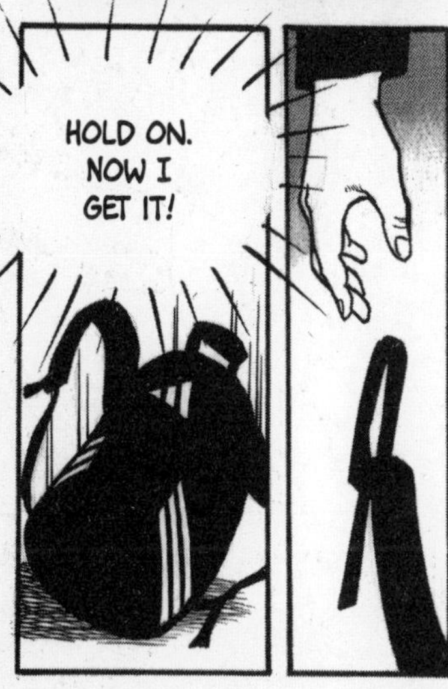
HOLD ON. NOW I GET IT!

THIS ISN'T A DREAM. JAPAN IS FOR REAL!
IT'S TIME FOR ME TO GET REAL!
つづく
(TO BE CONTINUED)

COMING SOON...

...THE ADVENTURE CONTINUES

He arrived in Japan as a 2nd-degree black belt, hoping to polish his karate skills before making a triumphant return home to win the national championship. But then he found out everything he thought to be true was just one big lie.

Stripped of his pride and busted back to a white belt, Sonny Leads has to prove himself all over again.

Is he up for the challenge? Will he fulfill the promises he's made to the stoic Ogami Sensei and best friend Kaz? Can he get Haruka's attention, never mind win her affection? And most important of all, will he learn to endure the humiliation of the playground *kancho* and actually experience all the magic Japan has to offer? Stay tuned!

Ready to learn even more Japanese?

Manga University's award-winning "Kanji de Manga" series makes learning how to read and write Japanese as fun and easy as picking up your favorite comic.

We start you out with "Kana de Manga," which uses easy-to-understand illustrations to teach you hiragana and katakana, the "ABCs of Japanese."

Learn over 800 characters and expressions!

After you've mastered kana, you're ready to take on the meat of the Japanese writing system: kanji. The six volumes in the "Kanji de Manga" series will teach you new words and expressions through manga-style comic strips.

"A brilliant idea!" says UCLA Japan studies Professor Ronald A. Morse. "Japanese kanji—the written symbols adapted from Chinese—were originally drawings of images from real life. Japanese comic books now provide fresh images to help us learn. Kanji de Manga uses today's manga images to make the kanji learning process fun and easy for students of all ages.."

On sale at fine bookstores worldwide. Also available in ebook editions through the Amazon Kindle Store, the Apple iBooks Store, Google Play, the Barnes & Noble Nook Store, and the Rakuten/Kobo Store. Or, purchase directly from our website at www.mangauniversity.com.

Page 95

ガサ (gasa)
Rummaging
through backpack

Page 98

グビッ
Same as page 39

プハーッ (puhaa)
Exhale after taking a drink

バン
Hard slap (on back)

Page 99

グビ
Same as page 39

ワハハハ
Same as page 19

ヒック (hikku)
Hiccup

Page 103

パンッ (pan)
Loud clap in unison
(signifying the end
of the party)

パチパチ
Same as page 89

Page 104

ドウッ (dou)
Drunken stumble

アハハ
Same as page 22

Page 105

シャシャッ (sha-sha)
Swish (as Taro's shuriken
slice through the air)

ピシピシ (pipi)
Shuriken striking their target

カチッ (kachi)
Click

パッ (pa)
Burst of light

Page 106

ワアアアア
Same as page 9

Page 108

つづく
"Tsuzuku"
To be continued
(note at bottom of page)

アチョーッ (achō)
Kung fu battle cry

バタッ (bata)
tumble

Page 88

居酒屋
"izakaya"
Bar and Grill
(written on paper lantern)

あいあい
"Ai Ai"
Name of izakaya
written on the curtains
at the entrance and on
the sign to the
left of the entrance

ビール
"Biiru" (beer)
Written at the
bottom of the sign to the
left of the entrance

メニュー
"Menyuu" (menu)
Written on
the sign to the right
of the entrance

ガヤガヤ (gaya-gaya)
Loud conversation

ブルル (bururu)
Buzz (vibrating cell phone)

Page 89

オーッス
Same as page 28

グビ
Same as page 39

グビ (gubi)
Same as page 39

パチパチ (pachi-pachi)
Clapping
(Japanese partygoers
traditionally applaud after
taking their first drinks
following a toast)

グビ
Same as page 39

Page 90

ムグムグ (mugu-mugu)
Munch-munch

Page 91

ブルル
Same as page 88

Page 93

ガシャン (gashan)
Glass shattering

Page 78

ドッ
Same as page 27

Page 79

ドッ
Same as page 27

ガクッ (gaku)
crumple

Page 80

バシッ
Same as page 29

ドッ
Same as page 27

Page 81

ツ (tsu)
Foot shuffle

ツツ (tsu-tsu)
Foot shuffle repeated

スッ (su)
Dodged punch

ドン
Same as page 63

Page 82

ヌッ (nu)
Sudden appearance

ドオッ (dō)
Bam (hard fall)

Page 84

ぎょうざ
"Gyouza"
(potstickers)
Restaurant sign

コーヒー
"Kōhii"
(coffee)
Cafe sign

タッ (da)
Footstep

サッ (sa)
Sudden appearance

和民
"Watami"
Name of restaurant on sign

ハルカ
"Haruka"
(Girl's name on uniform)

Page 85

夢 Cafe
"Yume (Dream) Cafe"
(sign behind Chie)

Page 86

バキュン (bakyun)
pow, bang (from a gun)

バシ
Same as page 29

Page 73

バシッ
Same as page 29

グッ
Same as page 71

Page 74

バタン
Same as page 44

ドターッ (dotaa)
Collapse onto floor

チュー (chuu)
Squeaky sip

バシュッ (bashu)
Swish

Page 75

バシッ (bashi)
Swish

バッ
Same as page 31

サッ (sa)
Posing sound

スゥーッ (suuu)
Slow posing

Page 76

タアアン (taaan)
Swish (while spinning in air)

ダッ (da)
Thud as foot hits ground

バッ
Same as page 31

だあぁっ (daaa)
Karate battle cry

Page 77

バッ
Same as page 31

バッ
Same as above

CONSONANTS ARE PRETTY MUCH THE SAME AS IN ENGLISH EXCEPT THE "F" SOUND, WHICH IS MUCH SOFTER, AND "R", WHICH FALLS BETWEEN A "D" AND AN "L".

Page 66

ギク (giku)
Doh!

バッ (ba)
Thud

アハハハ
Same a Page 22

ハアーイ (haaai)
Yay!

Page 67

山田
"Yamada"
(Name on uniform)

ポン (pon)
Removal of cap from hanko

ペタ (peta)
Stamping form with hanko

山田
"Yamada"
(Name stamped onto form)

Page 68

名前　　印
サニー
(The kanji for the words "name" and "stamp" are written in the top row of the form, above Sonny's name in katakana)

Page 69

キッ (ki)
squeak of car brakes

Page 70

ギシッ (gishi)
Creak of floorboards

大神道場
"Ogami Dojo"
(Dojo name on uniform)
Although only "Ogami" can be seen in this illustration, the full name (or other parts of it) can be seen in other illustrations.

Page 71

ガシッ (gashi)
Grab

グイッ (gui)
Pull

グッ (gu)
Sharp shove

バシッ
Same as page 29

Page 72

バシッ
Same as page 29

スッ (su)
Glide across floor

バババッ (baba)
Rapid air-karate punches

Page 50

メダル
"Medaru"
Medals (written on box)

Page 53

ぐああああ (guaaaa)
Snore

Page 56

第二００六二号
"Dai nisen rokuju ni gou"
Association No. 20062
(number on certificate)

Page 57

キッ (ki)
Squeal of tires

Page 58

ブロロ (buroro)
Vroom (car engine)

Page 61

アハハ
Same as page 22

Page 62

シュッシュッ (shu-shu)
Same as page 46

ピシッ
Same as page 12

Page 63

ガシッ (gashi)
Clasp hands

ムキ (muki)
Flex muscle

ドン (don)
Whomp

Page 64

グサッ (gusa)
Very strong poke

Page 65

ワアアアア (waaaa)
Noise of excited children

一日一善
"Ichi nichi ichi zen"
A proverb meaning "Do one good deed every day"
(scroll on classroom wall)

Page 43

ブォー (buō)
Rumble of car engine

トイレ
"Toire"
Toilet (sign on door)

ウィィン (uiin)
Automatic toilet seat lifting

Page 44

タロウ
"Taro"
(sign on Taro's bedroom door)

空手道
"Karatedo"
Karate Club (poster on wall)

ドン (don)
Shove

バタン (batan)
Door slam

Page 45

ヒロ
"Hiro"
(name written on boxes)

Page 46

シュッシュッ (shu-shu)
Whoosh (air karate)

Page 47

ダン (dan)
Click of door handle

バタン
Same as page 44

段位証書
"Dan i shou sho"
Dan Class Certificate
(written on tube)

Page 48

バ...
Same as page 31

A SMALL TSU (っ OR ッ)
IS OFTEN PUT AT THE END
OF A SOUND WORD TO ADD EMPHASIS,
LIKE AN EXCLAMATION MARK IN
ENGLISH. YOU DON'T ACTUALLY
PRONOUNCE IT.

Page 37

ハァーイ (haai)
Hi!

Page 38

フガ
Same as page 34

Page 39

フンッ (fun)
Humph

ガハハハ (gahahaha)
Wild laughter

グビ (gubi)
Gulp

Page 40

ゴンッ (gon)
Thump

はっはっはっ (hahaha)
Boisterous laughter

Page 41

きゃぁぁぁ (kyaaa)
Grossed out

プーン (puun)
Stench, stinky

フガ
Same as page 34

Page 42

バッ (ba)
Fabric being pulled from bag

シュワッチ (shuwachi)
The iconic sound made when Japan's beloved superhero Ultraman strikes his trademark "Shuwatch" battle pose

フガ
Same as page 34

THE JAPANESE LANGUAGE HAS 5 VOWEL SOUNDS: *A* AS IN *AH*, *I* AS IN *WE*, *U* AS IN *SOON*, *E* AS IN *GET*, AND *O* AS IN *OLD*.

Page 30 (cont.)

フゥーッ
Same as page 24

Page 31

バッ (ba)
Swoosh (from an air punch)

パッ (pa)
Dodged punch

Page 32

ダッ (da)
Forward thrust

ビシ
Same as page 27

ドッ (do)
Thump (from fall)

ダッ
Same as above

Page 33

ドンッ (don)
Hard kick

ビシ
Same as page 27

Page 34

パ (pa)
Hit face

パン (pan)
Hit face harder

バッ (ba)
Tissue being pulled from box

ギュッ (gyu)
Stuffing tissue into nose

フガ (fuga)
Sniffle of runny nose

だあっ (daa)
Yelling in the background

Page 35

バタン (batan)
Car door being closed

ギュギュッ (gyu-gyu)
Tires on pavement

田中
"Tanaka"
(family name on front door)

キッ (ki)
Car coming to a stop

Page 36

ガバッ (gaba)
Waking and sitting up

ガン (gan)
Smack

ピンポーン (pinpon)
Ding-dong (of doorbell)

Page 23

拳行人手唐
"Karatejingyouken"
An idiom that instructs karateka to think about nothing but karate when training at a dojo (sign inside dojo; the kanji are written and read right to left)

Page 24

フウーッ (fuuu)
Sigh

Page 25

クスクス (kesu-kesu)
Whisper, giggling

ドドッ (dodo)
Pop, pow (from punches, kicks)

Page 26

ピシッ
Same as page 12

Page 27

ビシ (bishi)
Whoosh (sharp jab)

ドッ (do)
Thwump (from a hard punch)

パパン (papan)
Double punch

Page 28

キィーッ (kiii)
Squeak of bicycle brakes

オーッス (ōssu)
Karate greeting

Page 29

ダァーッ (daaa)
Karate battle cry

ダン (dan)
Stomp

バシッ (bashi)
Whoosh (from a punch or kick)

ザッ (za)
Snap of dogi fabric as karateka move forward

Page 30

武練文修
"Shuubunrenbu"
An idiom imploring athletes to develop both their physical and mental skills (sign inside dojo; the kanji are written and read right to left)

Page 14

魂
"Tamashii"
Spirit (kanji on jacket)
ビッ (bi)
Bandage peel

Page 15

プッ
Chuckle

Page 16

フアー (fuaa)
Yawn

Page 18

ガァッ (gaa)
Skateboard on pavement

ガキーン (gakiin)
Skateboard tumbling

ダッ (da)
Footstep

Page 19

ワハハハ (wahahaha)
Laughter

Page 21

ダンス　空手道　ヨガ
師範
鈴木七段
"Dansu Karatedo Yoga"
"Shihan"
"Suzuki Nanadan"
Dance, Karate, Yoga
Master Suzuki, 7th Dan
(sign in dojo window)

Page 22

ドッ (do)
Running, stampede

ギャハハ (gyahaha)
Laughter

キャハハ (kyahaha)
Laughter

アハハ (ahaha)
Laughter

MOST SOUND EFFECTS ARE WRITTEN IN *KATAKANA*, BUT SOME SPOKEN SOUND EFFECTS ARE IN *HIRAGANA*, OR OCCASIONALLY *KANJI*.

Page 7

キィィィン (kiiin)
Whine of jet engines

ザンッ (zan)
Plane landing

ザワザワ (waza-waza)
Chatter, crowd noise

Page 8

魂
"Tamashii"
Spirit (kanji on T-shirt)

Page 9

ジロ (jiro)
staring

ワァアアァ (waaaa)
Roar of the crowd

Page 10

パァン (paan)
Smack, bang

Page 11

ワァアア
Same as page 9

Page 12

ピシッ (pishi)
Whack

Page 13

ワァアアア
Same as page 9

ペッ (pe)
Spitting out mouthguard

DID YOU KNOW THAT WRITTEN JAPANESE USES THREE DIFFERENT KINDS OF CHARACTERS? THEY'RE CALLED *HIRAGANA, KATAKANA* AND *KANJI.*

SOUND FX and TRANSLATIONS

Sonny Leads has a lot more to learn about Japan than just karate. If he's going to survive his homestay, truly interact with the locals and develop a deep understanding of Japanese society, he has to improve his language skills.

Many of the illustrations in this book feature sound effects and signs written in Japanese. Study this glossary along with Sonny, and you too can learn some Japanese!

Unlike the manga, this glossary and the other bonus material are organized from left page to right, so you should read and turn the pages the same way you would with any other English-language book. Each entry features a word or phrase written in Japanese, and its pronunciation in parentheses or translation in quotation marks, followed by the English-language equivalent (or explanation).

If a sound effect appears more than once, subsequent entries refer back to the original entry.

The following companies are leading suppliers of authentic Japanese dogi, gloves and other karate essentials.

Hirota Co., Ltd.
株式会社ヒロタ
NS Bldg. 1F 5-33-6 Kamata, Ota-ku, Tokyo 144-0052
Phone: 03-3730-5366
www.karategi-hirota.co.jp

Shureido Co., Ltd.
株式会社守礼堂
Greenforest Building 1F,
2-23-4 Nakano, Nakano-ku, Tokyo 164-0001
Phone: 03-5342 3051
www.shureido-karate.com

Tokaido Co., Ltd.
株式会社東海堂
Daiichi Misawa Building 3F, 1-15-2 Hongo,
Bunkyo-ku, Tokyo 113-0033
Phone: 03-5844-3451
www.tokaidojapan.com

Tokyodo International Co., Ltd.
(株) 東京堂インターナショナル
1-10-9 Yanagibashi, Taito-ku, Tokyo 111-0052
Phone: 03-3866-2997
www.tokyodo-in.co.jp

CHAMP Co. Ltd.
株式会社チャンプ

4-19-3-2F Koenji-Minami, Suginami-ku, Tokyo, 166-0003
Phone: 03-3315-3190

http://www.champ-shop.com/
http://www.jkfan.jp/jp/
http://www.karatedo.co.jp/

CHAMP Co., Ltd. is the publisher of JKFan Karate Magazine, the country's most popular periodical dedicated to the karate community. The publisher's mission is to contribute to the development of karate, both in Japan and internationally. Each monthly issue of JKFan is packed with articles, photographs and expert analysis as the magazine's reporters travel the globe to write about top athletes, instructors and the newest karate techniques. CHAMP also produces a lineup of karate DVDs, books and active wear, including the popular "OSS!" T-shirt pictured below.

Kenzen Sports Karate

4353 W Saanich Rd, Victoria, BC V8Z 3E9, Canada
Phone: 250-507-1441 (Canada)

http://www.kenzensportskarate.com

Kenzen Sports Karate is the newest organization in this directory, and is also the only one not located in Japan. Its roots, however, run deep in the birthplace of karate.

Co-founded by Kraig Devlin, a Canadian National Team coach with 30 years of karate experience, and "Sonny Leads" author Richard Mosdell, Kenzen Sports Karate offers members the opportunity to achieve the high standards set by the world-famous JKF Wadokai Karate Federation of Japan.

Kenzen is an athlete-centered, coach-driven, parent-supported performance training center. We believe that high-performance is an attitude and that inside each individual is an excellent, focused athlete waiting to be discovered. Both our competing and non-competing members are rarely willing to settle for anything less from themselves.

And soon, in conjunction with Manga University's Homestay Program, Kenzen Sports Karate will be offering karate tour-and-training excursions to Japan.

If you are in British Columbia, don't miss out on this opportunity to take the next step toward karate excellence. Contact Kenzen Sports Karate today.

Maeda Karate Club
明空義塾

1-48-2 2F Akabane Kita-ku, Tokyo 115-0045
Phone: 03-3901-9070

w01.tp1.jp/~a900219571/branch_office_meiku2011.htm

Toshiaki Maeda Sensei, a 1980 -65kg men's individual kumite WUKO world champion, served as the official JKF National Team Head Coach from from 2001 to 2007. Maeda Sensei is "Sonny Leads" author Richard Mosdell's direct instructor and one-time homestay father.

Shiramizu Karate Club
白水修養会館

707-1 Shimodakano,
Sugitomachi, Kita-Katsushikagun, Saitama
Phone: 0480-33-7205

http://homepage3.nifty.com/shiramizu/

Takamasa Arakawa Sensei runs the 400-plus-member Shiramizu dojo in Saitama Prefecture, just north of Tokyo. Arakawa Sensei is the best Japanese friend of "Sonny Leads" author Richard Mosdell, and he is also very popular with Wadokai overseas branch members.

If visiting Japan to practice at a Wadokai dojo, it is customary to visit the Shiramizu dojo and be the lucky recipient of their amazing kindness. Shiramizu also had a non-Japanese internship karate program from 2005-2011.

JKF Junior High School League

全国中学校空手道連盟

http://www.jjkf.net

Like the university and high school leagues, the junior high league has national, regional and local events. Junior high schools also now must teach all their students a budo art, with the principal of each school normally picking karate, kendo or judo. Most top junior high athletes began their training in a private dojo while still in elementary school.

Seiritsu HS Karate Club

成立学園空手道部

6-9-13 Higashi-Jujo, Kita-ku, Tokyo 114-0001
Phone: 0120-958810

http://www.seiritsu.ac.jp

The Seiritsu club is the oldest high school karate club in Tokyo, having been founded in 1963. The author of "Sonny Leads," Richard Mosdell, was the club's head coach from March 2005 to April 2014.

Elementary School Competitions

There are also a few local and national events for elementary school athletes, though these competitions are not as prevalent as those for older students. In general, elementary school students compete in local open and style-only events separated into grade-age categories.

JKF High School League
全国高等学校体育連盟空手道部

www.jkf-hs.com

The Kotairen is another national league made up of the regional leagues, which themselves are composed of the city leagues to which high school karate clubs belong.

Japanese students attend high school for 3 years, with two and a half of those years spent practicing in the karate club an average of five or six days a week. There are usually five local events each year that are qualifiers for very competitive regional and national events.

Non-Japanese exchange students in Japan can enter these tournaments through a high school club they join.

JKF Inter-High
全国高等学校体育連盟空手道部

The Inter-High is an annual mini-Olympics for high school students of all sports. The event is held each August, with a different prefecture hosting the event every year.

In the karate competition, usually only the top one or two karate competitors and kumite teams from each city league are able to qualify.

Overseas visitors will find the Inter-High, which takes place at the height of the summer holiday season, to be very festive. The karate events are highly competitive, as a good result can lead to an invitation to a top university club.

JKF University League
全日本学生空手道連盟

www.jukf.org

Many universities in Japan have karate clubs that belong to the JKF University League, and four-year undergraduates constitute most of the membership.

The friends one makes in university, especially in a club, tend to be their friends for life. Many non-Japanese attend Japanese undergraduate and graduate school programs taught in both Japanese and English, and they are allowed to join this league through a university club.

Takushoku University Karate Club
拓殖大学空手部

www.karate.ne.jp/takushoku/

Takudai is a famous karate club from which many Shotokan instructors have attended. One of the main coaches now is Richard Heselton, who has lived in Japan for decades and captained the club when he was a Takudai undergraduate, making him probably the first non-Japanese to captain a university karate club.

All-Japan Businessmen Karatedo Federation
全日本実業団空手道連盟

6-18 Hikarigaoka 2-chome, Kashiwa-shi, Chiba 277-0065
Phone: 090-9852-2686

www.wkf.jp/ajbkf/
ajbkf@wkf.jp

There are many small and large businesses in Japan with their own karate dojo, and these can join the All-Japan Businessmen Karatedo Federation so their employees can compete in tournaments. If someone is working in Japan, they can request their company register them with the federation so that they may participate in tournaments and seminars.

The federation in an alliance of three organizations: the East Japan Businessmen Karatedo Federation, the West Japan Businessmen Karatedo Federation, and the Japan Self-Defense Forces Karatedo Federation.

All three pride themselves on fostering budo culture within both private and public corporations, and many of their members have enjoyed success in regional and national tournaments.

Nippon Budokan
日本武道館

2-3 Kitanomaru-Koen, Chiyoda-ku, Tokyo 102-8321
Phone: 03-3216-5144
Fax: 03-3216-5156

www.nipponbudokan.or.jp

The iconic Nippon Budokan arena and attached training halls are a legacy building and budo organization from the 1964 Tokyo Summer Olympics.

The nine main modern budo arts (karate, judo, kendo, sumo, shorinji kempo, aikido, naginata, jyukendo and kyudo) all belong to the organization, and many budo groups hold their national championships there.

With its octagonal arena and storied history, the Nippon Budokan is a must-see facility for both the budo practitioner and the casual traveler.

International Seminar of Budo Culture
国際武道文化セミナー

Every March, the Nippon Budokan's education division hosts a three-day weekend of budo lectures and practice sessions at its training retreat center in Katsuura, Chiba Prefecture. Non-Japanese dan rank holders living in Japan are among the invited participants.

Tokyo Karatedo Association
東京都空手道連盟

2-14-4-201 Asagaya-kita, Suginami-ku, Tokyo 166-0001
Phone: 03-3223-9002

http://www.tokuren.jp

While the JKF has branch groups at the prefectural and city levels, Tokyo has its own prefectural karate association because it is both the capital and the largest population center in Japan.

都 空 連

Local Tokyo clubs join the Tokuren from their many city areas (each with their own area karate federation) and the Tokuren hosts tournaments, seminars, dan tests and officials' seminars as the JKF's local representative organization.

The long-term visitor to Japan will not only join a private club and the style organization the club belongs too, but usually will also join both the national JKF and the prefectural JKF groups (in this case, the Tokuren) so that they can participate in all the open-style events the JKF offers from the city to national level.

Okinawa Traditional Karate Liaison Bureau
沖縄伝統空手総合案内ビューロー

1-25-25 Ameku, Naha City, Okinawa 900-0005
+81-98-851-3669 (please call before visiting the office)

www.okkb.org

This organization offers overseas visitors the opportunity to train in Okinawa, the birthplace of karate, and experience traditional karate or kobudo with local masters. Contact the bureau with your travel plans and it will strive to arrange for you a training session or a visit in a dojo of the cradle of karate.

Kokutai
国民体育大会 空手道競技

Kokutai is short for "national citizen tournament," which is a mini-Olympics of many sports for adults. The event is held each September, with a different prefecture hosting the event every year.

The athletes who compete in the karate competition have qualified by winning their prefecture competitions.

Non-Japanese who live in Japan can compete in Kokutai as well by qualifying in their prefectures' JKF all-styles annual championships.

JKF Wadokai
全日本空手道連盟和道会

Uematsu Bldg. 7F 1-9-2,
Nishi-Shinbashi, Minato-ku, Toyko 105-0003
Phone: 03-3595-0100
Fax: 03-3595-1040
www.karatedo.co.jp/wado/w_eng/e_index.htm (English)
www.karatedo.co.jp/wado (Japanese)

Of the several style organizations for the Wadoryu style, the JKF Wadokai is the official Wado-style group within the Japan Karate Federation.

As the original Wado-style organization and the largest, it has expanded both in Japan and worldwide by its many instructors. Only JKF Wadokai members use the name "Wadokai" and its iconic dove-and-fist logo.

Guseikai Karatedo
偶成会高木道場

2-6-13 5F Takagi Dental Office,
Kita-Otsuka, Toshima-ku, Tokyo 170-0004
Phone: 03-3949-0563

Hideo Takagi Sensei is an 8th dan in both the Wadokai and the JKF. Widely recognized as one of the most naturally adept Wado-style practitioners, Takagi Sensei is popular with both Japanese and overseas members.

JKF Shitokai
全日本空手道連盟糸東会

3-8-11 Hamazaki Asakashi, Saitama-ken, 351-0033
Phone: 048-476-3818
Fax: 048-476-3869

www.karatedo.co.jp/shitokai/English/et-index.html (English)
www.karatedo.co.jp/shitokai (Japanese)

Of the several style organizations for the Shitoryu style, the JKF Shitokai is the official Shito-style group within the Japan Karate Federation.

World Shitoryu Karatedo Federation

www.karatedo.co.jp/shitokai/wskf/index.html

The JKF Shitokai oversees the World Shitoryu Karatedo Federation, which was founded by JKF Shitokai in 1993 and serves Shitoryu associations in more than 55 countries and territories.

JKF Gojukai

全日本空手道連盟剛柔会

2-21-6-808 Higashi-Ikebukuro, Toshima-ku, Tokyo 170-0013
Phone: 03-5951-1165

www.karatedo.co.jp/gojukai/english

Of the several organizations for the Gojuryu style, the JKF Gojukai is the official Goju-style group within the Japan Karate Federation.

International Karatedo Gojukai Association

国際空手道剛柔会

1-16-23 Zenpukuji, Suginami-ku, Tokyo 167-0041
Phone: 03-3395-2311

http://gojukaikaratedo.com

The International Karatedo Gojukai Association is a Goju-style organization founded by the late Gogen Yamaguchi that has branches on five continents. The headquarters is located in Tokyo and one of its senior instructors is a close associate of "Sonny Leads" author Richard Mosdell.

Shotokan Karatedo International Federation (SKIF)
国際松濤館空手道連盟

2-1-20 Minami Kugahara, Ota-ku, Tokyo 146-0084
Phone: 03-3754-5481

www.skifworld.com
skif-ghq@skif.jp (overseas inquiries)
skif@skif.jp (Japanese inquiries)

Hirokazu Kanazawa, chief instructor of the Shotokan Karate-do International Federation, is arguably the most famous Shotokan instructor in the world. He has taught in dozens of countries, and he has many fans both inside and outside the Shotokan community.

SKIF has grown to become one of the most vibrant karate organizations both within Japan and internationally.

Kanazawa Sensei's dojo is conveniently located between Tokyo and Yokohama.

Japan Karate Association (JKA)
公益社団法人日本空手協会

2-23-15 Koraku, Bunkyo-ku, Tokyo 112-0004
Phone: 03-5800-3091

www.jka.or.jp

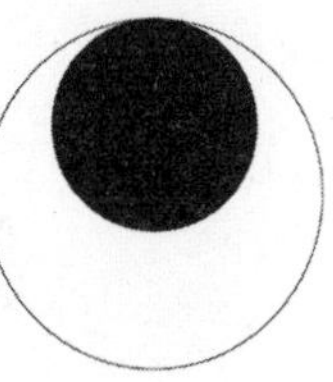

The JKA is the largest Shotokan organization in Japan, and probably throughout the world. While there are several Shotokan-style organizations each with their own vision for the performance of this style, the JKA's large membership and inter-style activities make it a very vibrant karate community.

JKA is also famous for its Instructor's Program (Kenshusei "internship" program), which runs for one year at the JKA headquarters in Tokyo, and from which professional instructors are trained.

For the visitor to Japan interested in Shotokan karate, a JKA dojo is normally the easiest to find.

The JKF National Championships

While there are many national championships in Japan for different karate styles and leagues, the Japan Nationals for individual adult kata and kumite divisions is held at the Nippon Budokan in Tokyo the first Sunday of every December.

The top athletes from every prefecture, plus returning champions and champions of other leagues that year, such as the university league, participate. Those who perform well in this tournament are invited to official National Team selection events.

For the visitor to Japan, this tournament and the prefecture team kumite nationals that are held a day earlier at the Tokyo Budokan in Ayase are must-see events. One ticket covers admission to both events, making it a real bargain.

The JKF National Team

The athletes selected for the National Junior and Senior Team represent Japan at international events, which include the WKF World Senior Championships, WKF World Junior & Cadet Championships, the AKF Asian Karate Championships, the WKF World University Championships and the World Games.

Japan Karatedo Federation (JKF)
全日本空手道連盟

1-1-20 Tatsumi, Koto-ku, Tokyo 135-8538
Phone: 03-5534-1951

www.karatedo.co.jp/jkf/jkf-eng/e_index.htm (English)
www.jkf.ne.jp (Japanese)

The Japan Karatedo Federation (JKF) is the official umbrella body of most mainstream karate in Japan. There are branches for towns and prefectures, as well as high school and university leagues, all the way from local to national levels.

The official national teams of Japan are also organized through the JKF. Athletes visiting Japan from overseas can interact with the JKF by registering with a local club and competing in an all-styles JKF event at the local level, as well as by taking a JKF all-styles dan or officials test.

The JKF main website has a calendar that lists the main karate community events for the year.

JKF Dan Tests

If you hold a dan rank up to 3rd dan from one of the four main karate JKF style organizations, then you can apply for an equivalent JKF dan rank without a test. From 4th dan up, a test is required, which is seen within the karate community as the standard for all dan ranks regardless of one's style dan rank.

JKF
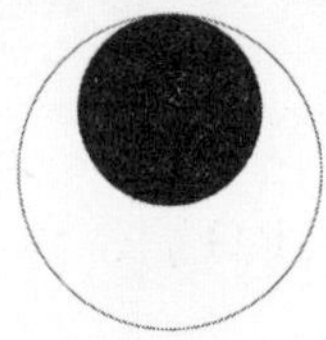

SHOTOKAN·KARATE-DO·INTERNATIONAL
国際松濤館空手道連盟

JKF
剛柔会

空手道

都
空
連

I.K.G.A.

実

CHAMP

OKAIDO

HIROTA

空手衣・空手用品専門店
SHUREIDO

TOKYODO
INTERNATIONAL

SPECIALIZING IN AUTHENTIC MARTIAL ARTS EQUIPMENT
Natural
Simple
Life
JAPAN

JAPAN KARATE DIRECTORY

Karate originated as a hand-to-hand combat system in the Ryuku Kingdom (which comprised the islands now known as Okinawa) during the 14th century. In the 1920s and 1930s, the martial art expanded to the Japanese mainland, and then from there to all parts of the country. Karate's growth exploded with the "karate boom" from the 1950s onwards, to the point where karate can now be found in every country on the globe.

Mainstream karate is considered to be the different style associations (Wado, Shotokan, Shito, Goju and Genseiryu and Rengokai) that interact with one another through the numerous national, regional and local branches of the Japan Karatedo Federation (JKF). Non-mainstream Kyokushin karate also enjoys immense popularity, with organizations throughout Japan.

Foreign karateka coming to Japan to improve their techniques are encouraged to find a dojo whose instructor is not only knowledgeable and professional, but also friendly and inviting. The dojo's Japanese members should be welcoming of overseas visitors, too.

The Japanese organizations, tournaments, seminars, clubs and equipment suppliers listed on the following pages all foster the spirit and development of karate as a both a cherished national heritage and an internationally revered sport.

The one suggestion I have for any high school karate club is to take their club to an international event every three years so that every student can experience karate with non-Japanese at least once while they are in high school. An ideal event to attend would be the International Hawaiian Open Championships in November. Many nationalities gather there and the competitors tend to be of high caliber, so new ideas, strategies and tactics can be learned firsthand. Plus, there may be a way to arrange a training camp after the tournament with other interested teams.

The question I sometimes get from non-Japanese international students is whether high school karate clubs will accept them. The answer is yes. International students training within their school's karate club is a great way to learn Japanese, make friends, and have a far deeper experience in Japan. It is also beneficial for the Japanese students, as they make international friends through whom they can build an international viewpoint. Truly through karate the world can become closer.

keep up their practices, to fight the "good fight," build the reputation of the school and honor their predecessors with strong competitive results. Wonderful. It's hard for me not to shed a few tears.

Fall arrives with tournaments to qualify for Nationals. I warmly remember the first time as their coach our club qualified for Nationals. Just a few days later, a four-story banner announcing our achievement hung from the top of the school's main building. How cool is that?! I felt a real sense of pride that our accomplishments, and hundreds of squats, had paid off!

Winter before Nationals of course brings the cold Siberian winds over Japan. In Canada in winter we need to turn on the heat in the dojo, as it can get as low as -35 degrees Celsius in some cities. But even though it seldom falls below zero in Tokyo, I was surprised to see how so many dojo don't use heaters in the winter at all, as students wear their club track suits under their dogi to stay warm for the first part of the training. This reminds me of the saying, "In the West we heat the house, but in Japan we heat the body."

The atmosphere at Nationals is very serious. Everyone — from athletes to coaches to officials to volunteers to spectators — clutches programs and acts like they have a job to do that is integral to the championship. Just like overseas, an athlete's and a club's reputation can be cemented at Nationals in Japan. I was surprised to see such a high level of ability from the students. So when I'm standing with my athletes in the middle of the arena beside the mat as they compete, I always think there is no other place I want to be but right here. Actually, being in the dojo everyday is the most enjoyable thing for me, but when it leads to the Nationals, like in any country, it is something truly to look forward to.

"quiet and reserved" gets thrown out the window when a non-Japanese sees a high school karate club practice! At any time during standing basics, moving basics or kumite practice, everyone hollers kiai. Even the students waiting in line continue to kiai to keep the energy up. Everyone is constantly yelling encouragement and advice, so it gets pretty noisy. I think this is great — it makes me feel 20 years younger, too!

Even more intensive than daily practice is summer camp. When spoken aloud, those two words — "summer camp" — seem to weigh heavy on the minds of the Japanese, who will become quiet and reflective. Karate summer camp in Japan is the hardest, toughest time of the year, especially when compared to many overseas camps that are a mixture of training and leisure time. Here, everyone eats together, trains together, sleeps together and bathes together. There's before-breakfast practice, morning practice and afternoon practice, plus nighttime lectures and note taking. For four straight days, and sometimes even more. The first time I attended one of these camps, my thoughts of playing beach volleyball every afternoon disappeared really fast!

Discipline is meted out differently, too. Whereas overseas we normally order pushups if the students make a glaring mistake in practice, I was surprised to discover at summer camp that a common training punishment is 100 squats, meaning more than 1,000 squats can be required a day. It's not unusual to see students actually crawling out of the dojo with leg cramps at the end of a session. Rough. But this is great at the same time because such an exercise builds the spirit as well as the body.

What I find charming at summer camp is how after a new captain is elected, the third-years who have just retired each give a speech to their kohai (juniors) asking them to began wiping the mirrors. This is how I learned that the first-years do all the chores. Interesting, I thought to myself. Maybe they'll wash my car too...

One of the biggest differences for me coaching in Japan compared to Canada was how my training menu had to adjust to the needs to the club. I'm used to two to three hours of daily competitive, strategic training (footwork, tactical theory depending on point score, adjusting attack plans when facing stronger, even or weaker opponents), and maybe only two times a week of training the basics. But here the students really wanted an hour or more of just basics every day to feel they're ready before competitive training. Yet that's OK, as it has become possible to balance both training menus since the students come to the dojo six days a week, compared to three or four times a week overseas. It's similar to a professional modern ballet company that still has classical lessons in the morning for the dancers to keep developing their skills prior to their practice of avant-garde productions in the afternoon.

One thing a karate club in Japan is really good at is building intensity. The stereotypical view that Japanese are

High School Karate in Japan Through a Non-Japanese Coach's Eyes

By Richard Mosdell

Huge colorful cloth banners drape from the spectator balcony that wraps around the arena, each banner blazingly declaring its club's motto, such as "Never Give Up!" or "Eat the bark off a tree to survive!" Hundreds of karate-uniformed high school students march in military lines, swinging their arms high, as high school girls in their skirted uniforms lead each team while holding placards announcing the clubs' names. The teams file by the VIP stage at the front, where the many karate associations' presidents stand at attention. For a non-Japanese, it is an impressive display of the color and pageantry at the opening ceremony of the All-Japan Karate High School National Championships!

But to get to Nationals, I had to adjust to the Japanese high school karate club culture first. I remember one of the first times I went to clean the dojo at Tokyo's Seiritsu Gakuen, where I had just been made the new karate coach. A first-year student grabbed the mop out of my hand, bowed, and proceeded to mop the floor. Hmm. Then I tried to clean the mirrors, but another student grabbed the cloth, bowed, and

ABOUT THE ARTIST

GENSHI KAMOBAYASHI (born in 1955 in Miyazaki Prefecture) has been a manga artist and karateka for most of his life. He began his career in the early 1970s as an assistant to the mangaka Sei Narushima, a connection that later afforded Kamobayashi the opportunity to work on several popular series, including "Macross," "Future Boy Conan" and "Ultraman." He made his publishing debut in 1976 with "Niji ni Mukatte" ("Toward the Rainbow"), followed by "The Gorilla," a police-action manga he authored under the pen name Noboru Sakaoka. More recently, he has focused on sports comics, including "Karate no Tamago" (literally "Egg of Karate"), about a young person who dreams of being a star karate athlete. He also draws "Magic," a karate-themed manga that appears in each issue of JKFan Karate Magazine. He holds a 3rd dan in Shotokan Karate and a 3rd dan in Ryukyu Kobudo, and is a 4th dan Japan Karate Federation instructor. Every Friday he puts down his art pens and heads to the local community center, where he teaches karate to elementary and junior high school students.

Self-portrait by artist

ABOUT THE AUTHOR

RICHARD MOSDELL (5th dan JKF Wadokai) started learning karate in the 1980s, and then to broaden his study of it he lived in Japan a total of 11 years over various long-term stays since first arriving in 1993 as a Japanese Studies undergraduate from Canada. A student of various karate styles and a former sports karate athlete, he has spent over 25 years developing a career as a professional karate instructor, which included being the head coach of the oldest high school karate club in Tokyo (Seiritsu Gakuen) from 2005-2014. During this time Richard was a bilingual author for the famous JKFan Karate Magazine, while he completed a Masters in Global Studies at Sophia University, with his graduation thesis titled, "The Globalization of Karate." Richard was then accepted into the prestigious Tokyo University of Foreign Studies Peace & Conflict Studies Ph.D. program, and his research is titled, "Beyond Sport for Peace; the transformative results of learning karate as a vehicle for instilling human rights in post-conflict societies." In addition to writing his doctoral thesis, Richard is now a co-owner and professional coach of Kenzen Sports Karate, a high-performance karate training center in Victoria, Canada.

Illustration by Johnny Tesoro

Kazunori Kadota, Kenji Motonomi, Masato Miura, Eikin Yogo, Tomomi Udagawa, Hidehiro Makise, Ryoko Natsumi, Mayuko Matsuda, Misako Mochisue, Ken Akakura, Tsuya Nakamura, Seiko Yamamoto. *Seiritsu Soccer Club:* Satoshi Miyauchi, Yasuya Igarashi, Naoto Yoshida, Ikuya Yamada, Kotaro Morioka, Kenji Yamamoto, Masahiro Oota, Hitomi Sawaguchi, Nazomi Yamago, Michael Fitzgerald. *Sophia University Graduate Program in Global Studies:* David Wank, Koichi Nakano, Mari Miura, Tadashi Anno, James Farrer, Michio Hayashi, Chuanfei Wang. *Tokyo University of Foreign Studies Peace & Conflict Studies PhD Program:* Kenji Isezaki, Akito Okada, Jun Matsukuma, Rie Ishida. *JKF Tokyo High School Karate League:* Akira Kondo, Toshihisa Sofue, Shuji Kusaka, Hirofumi Momoida, Hideo Fukuda, Yuuki Nasa, Akiyoshi Kano, Takashi Iwasa, Kazuhide Yamashita, Hiroshi Maeda, Tomokuki Tezuka, Takeshi Hosogai, Haruto Okushima, Oichi Shimamura.

— Richard Mosdell

I would like to express my deepest gratitude to my family for their love, encouragement and patience; to my sensei, Sei Narushima, for his guidance and leadership; and, of course, to Richard Mosdell for allowing me the opportunity to participate in this very special project.

— Genshi Kamobayashi

Acknowledgments

First, a warm thank you to both Genshi Kamobayashi for bringing my story to life, and to *Manga University's* Glenn Kardy and Mari Oyama for believing so passionately in this project for so many years!

I want to thank the following people for putting up with me too! If I missed someone's name, you're probably sighing with relief. Seriously, I feel very lucky to have interacted with the people on this list, all of whom truly enriched my experiences that related to the writing of this book. Bonita Mosdell, Bill Mosdell, Jeff Mosdell, Edna Roe, Johnny Tesoro, Enid Ho, Kevin Floyd, Jen Lam, Mike Websdale, Dani Price, Nick Smith, Kyoko Smith, Pete Williams, Rich Heselton, Brent Regan, Don Sharp, Alexandre Franchi, Paul Atkin, Chee Ling, Reza Salmani, Koichi Nakano (Shiga), Robbie Smith. *CHAMP Co. Ltd./JKFan Karate Magazine:* Masahiro Ide, Aina Kobinata. *Kenzen Sports Karate:* Kraig Devlin, Anna Stein, Cathy Singleton Bowers, Leslie Bowers. *Canada Wadokai:* Norma Foster, Peter Stoddart, Bob Mooney, Lawrence Liang, Marta Adamovich, Frances Li, Sherri Collier, Brenda Painter, Catherine Wood, Dharmesh Dass, Steve Johnson, Erica Ip. *Meiku Gijuku Karate:* Toshiaki Maeda, Hidemi Wada, Satoshi Fujita, Masahiro Hori, Sora Kikuchi. *Shiramizu ShuyoKai Karate:* Takamasa Arakawa, Hiroyuki Uehara, Bunmei Suzuki, Hitoshi Kikuchi, Takamasa Iwasaki, Yukiko Yamazaki, Noriko Yoshihara, Shiori Koike, Keiko Arakawa, Rie Hirai. *Japan Wadokai:* Hideho Takagi, Katsumi Hakoishi, Toru Arakawa, Shigeru Kato, Shunsuke Yanagida, Shinji Kohata, Takuya Furuhashi, Koji Okumachi, Seiji Nishimura. *Seiritsu Gakuen Kindergarten, Junior High & High School:* Kohei Fukuda, Haruko Fukuda, Yohei Fukuda, Eiji Fukuda, Chieko Kawakami, Yumiko Monma, Kenichi Saijo, Masako Suzuki, Kiyotaka Akashi, Keiichiro Tanaka, Osamu Maruo, Yuko Akutsu, Tomomutsu Nogami, Hiroshi Kakiya,

ISBN 978-4-921205-34-8
eISBN 978-4-921205-81-2 (ebook)

First edition, June 2014

10 9 8 7 6 5 4 3 2 1 y 14 15 16 17 18 19 20

Printed in Canada

Manga University presents...
"Sonny Leads"
By Richard Mosdell
Illustrated by Genshi Kobayashi

Published by Manga University under the auspices of
Japanime Co. Ltd., 3-31-18 Nishi-Kawaguchi, Kawaguchi-shi, Saitama-ken
332–0021, Japan.

Publisher: Glenn Kardy
Art coordinator: Mari Oyama
Translator: Rie Mosdell
Production assistant: Jessica Shacklett
Editorial assistant: Raven Wells
Cover design: Jodi Heard

Special thanks to Ron and Judy Hibbard, Masahiro Ide, Aina Kobinata,
Minami Murakami, Edward Mazza, Adam Van Wyk, Hiroshi Kai,
Momoka Ishikawa, Ikuo Fukuyama, Naomi Rubin and Shinobu Sendai.

"Just asking means you are not ready to know."

Kana de Manga
144 pages / B&W / $9.99
ISBN 978-4-921205-01-0

Kanji de Manga Vol. 1
144 pages / B&W / $9.99
ISBN 978-4-921205-02-7

Kanji de Manga Vol. 2
144 pages / B&W / $9.99
ISBN 978-4-921205-03-4

Kanji de Manga Vol. 3
144 pages / B&W / $9.99
ISBN 978-4-921205-04-1

Kanji de Manga Vol. 4
144 pages / B&W / $9.99
ISBN 978-4-921205-09-6

Kanji de Manga Vol. 5
144 pages / B&W / $9.99
ISBN 978-4-921205-10-2

Kanji de Manga Vol. 6
144 pages / B&W / $9.99
ISBN 978-4-921205-11-9

Japanese Sound FX!
144 pages / B&W / $9.99
ISBN 978-4-921205-12-6

Yojijukugo
144 pages / B&W / $9.99
ISBN 978-4-921205-22-5

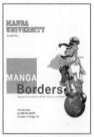

Other books available from Manga University

Manga Moods
96 pages / Color / $9.99
ISBN 978-4-921205-13-3

Manga Moods Too
96 pages / Color / $9.99
ISBN 978-4-921205-33-1

Manga University is the world's leading publisher of English-language instructional manga, including the award-winning *Manga Cookbook*, the *Kanji de Manga* series and the *Manga Moods* and *Manga Moods Too* collection.

For more info about these and other fine books, please visit our website at **manga-u.com**

50 Things We Love About Japan / $9.99
ISBN 978-4-921205-08-9

Manga Sisters
96 pages / Color / $9.99
ISBN 978-4-921205-18-8

Harvey & Etusko's Manga Guide to Japan / $9.99
ISBN 978-4-921205-17-1

Mimei's Hollywood (Japanese ed.) / $9.99
ISBN 978-4-921205-32-4

The Chrysanthemum and the Bat (ebook)
ISBN 978-4-921205-84-3

SENSEI SAYS...

THIS IS THE LAST PAGE!

JAPANESE MANGA ARE READ FROM RIGHT TO LEFT, THE OPPOSITE OF AMERICAN COMICS...
...AND JUST LIKE KARATE, READING RIGHT TO LEFT TAKES PRACTICE. BUT IT SOON FEELS QUITE NATURAL.
START AT THE TOP AND WORK YOUR WAY DOWN, *FROM RIGHT...*
...TO LEFT! SEE, IT'S NOT TOO DIFFICULT.

NOW, TURN THIS BOOK OVER TO READ THE ***FIRST*** PAGE!